Copyright © 2018 California State University Channel Islands;

All rights reserved.

TABLE OF CONTENTS

INTRODUCTION...1

FOREWORD..2

PART 1: CURRENT EOP STUDENTS....................3

    ORLANDO....................................3

    AYDEN..7

    ANGELINA..................................14

    MADDISON.................................22

    TIMBER.......................................27

    DEBBIE..29

    DONNA.......................................32

    EZRA..40

    LILIAN..47

    DREAM..54

    MARISOL.....................................62

    CHRISTOPHER...........................72

PART 2: EOP ALUMNI....................................85

    JUAN..86

XIMENA……………………………..95

MICHELLE………………………….101

LILO…………………………………..105

SOFIA………………………………..115

SARINA………………………………123

AARON………………………………135

GLOSSARY OF TERMS…………………………………..142

Educational Opportunity Program (EOP) Students' Autobiographies

In April 1969, the California Legislature passed Senate Bill 1072 (the Harmer Bill) which established EOP at California state institutions of higher learning. Nearly 50 years later, the EOP program is going strong, with access provided to first generation, low income, historically underserved students.

Foreword

EOP students from California State University Channel Islands wrote the following autobiographies. In an attempt to keep the authenticity of each student voice, minor grammatical edits occurred and alias names are used.

As the Assistant Director of EOP, I have heard these stories firsthand and countless additional stories that mirror many of the incidents and adversities documented here. I believe exposure to the histories of the students EOP serves will garner more support for this life-changing program.

Special thanks to these EOP students for sharing their story and offering a glimpse into their past.

Humbly,
Kari L. Moss
Assistant Director, EOP

ORLANDO

The best way to describe a personal life is to know where it all first began. I can only say that in the world I grew up, opportunities were priceless. I grew up in a town called Highland Park, a mid-sized community that was known for its gangs, over-populated family homes and shops, as well as a central location for all the cities surrounding Highland Park. Academically, I was pushed to achieve and succeed. I am grateful to the people who helped me build a foundation towards greater successes, yet they could not stop the number of obstacles and challenges that headed my way. My parents, who never had this kind of opportunity back in their homeland, were very strict that I did well in my schoolwork and that I made something of myself; it worked. Although they helped me succeed through high school, I had many other families outside my immediate family that helped me throughout my years. I was a part of a camp, R.M Pyles Boys Camp, which helped me grow morally into a leader. I learned how to shape a better tomorrow not just for myself, but also for the world I shared my life with. RM Pyles Boys Camp gave me the opportunity to give back. I was given a job and worked my way up, following the same mission my counselor followed before me. As significant as this is to me morally, programs such as Telacu, Upward Bound and the Educational Opportunity Program (EOP) have mentored me to succeed in my studies and to learn to network and connect with people to have a prosperous future. The road is never easy, as is said by everyone who faces their problems, but nobody should ever stop following the road that leads to a better life.

    If I was asked how I got myself this far, I could answer in one word: persistence. All of these influences as I came towards attending the university have molded, shaped, and created someone who has the skills to advocate, learn, teach, and inspire in order to share the same knowledge as is passed down for generations. Now, presently I am close to graduating from CSU Channel Islands, and I thank EOP and Pyles for supporting me in counsel and finance to achieve this accumulation of years of work. Working part-time for Conferences and Events has been a blessing thanks to EOP assistant director and awesome counselor. Here I am taking on the responsibilities of the real world that usually falls on someone once school is over. I find these challenges are good to learn at an early age, because from failure comes knowledge, and that can never be lost, because it is an experience that helps me get closer to achievement. I do admit that I may find stress and apathy when I am further out of school, but I know that I have great expectations from everyone who gave their efforts in helping me get this far. I would feel like I ripped them off after everything they have done for me. For those reasons, I hope these words can be relatable and helpful for anyone else to shape their own path to success and take on their own adventure.

"All we have to decide is what to do with the time that is given to us."

-J.R.R Tolkien

AYDEN

If one were to see my life as it is, they would think I had a normal family. I had a father, mother, older sister, and a family dog. However, in my life that is the surface of the situation. If one were to look into my life, they would find that my family has a deep problem with alcohol.

The problem that was always present in my family was alcohol in the form of my father's alcoholism. The first time I remember this being an issue was when I was four years old. My sister and I were crying on our couch because our drunk dad was arguing with my mom. I hated hearing them yell at each other, so I stood up and yelled at my dad, "Please, stop!" He responded by punching a hole in the wall and leaving. Like that hole, a deep impression was left. The hole is still there.

Growing up I never knew what alcohol was. The only thing I ever knew was that it was in beers which my dad drank a lot of. It was not so bad when I was younger. My father would probably get intoxicated once a month, and would ask me to come to his room where he would look at me give me a kiss on my head and tell me "I love you." If he said that, I knew he was drunk. That is probably why I do not feel anything now when he says it.

    His drinking became more and more frequent as I grew older. By the age of eight, it was probably twice a month now. The more he drank, the more I was careful to not say anything to disturb the peace of the house when he was drunk. I knew that if I stayed quiet he would not talk to me or my mom and would go to his room to sleep it off. I feel that being forced to be quiet had resulted in me being very quiet, timid and shy as a child. I thought that I could avoid problems if I stayed quiet.

Although it had always been a part of my life, it was not until midway of my junior year where I had enough of my father's alcoholic habits. So at 16, I went to him and I told him all the problems I have with his drinking, all the fear I have when he drinks, all the times I frustrated myself trying to speak up but being too afraid too, and all the times I hurt myself banging my head trying to figure out why I am living with this. After I told him, he left and went to get more beer. That was the day I realized my father loved alcohol more than me.

I did not really talk much with him after that. I was too busy with school waking up at 5 in the morning, riding my skateboard to school two miles away, taking seven advanced placement classes because the other classes that were offered were not beneficial, and getting back home at 8 PM. I kept myself busy with all the stress of school work. And for a time, even though I was exhausted, I was content with everything. Until, one day, my senior year of high school.

This one night my father was drunk. More drunk than I had ever seen him. And he was planning to leave the house and drive his car. I realized that if he goes, innocent people could get hurt. As when I was four years old, I stood up to my father. I tried to take the car keys away from him. In my attempt to take them away, he pulled the keys back. Suddenly, we were in a fight over them. When, in his drunk state, he pulled his arm away and as he did this he slashed the left side of my body and hit my neck, leaving a bruise. Luckily, it was not serious as I was not bleeding, but I had realized he had cut me. Realizing that my father had hurt me in his drunken state made me give up on him finally. After this night, I no longer see that man as my father. Since then, I talk to him minimally. He apologizes now and then but only when he is drunk. He has not stopped drinking. Even after everything, he blames me for his alcoholism. He believes that because I do not see him as my father, he drinks.

Since coming to CSU Channel Islands, and more importantly EOP, my life has turned for the better. I am accomplishing more than I had ever thought possible. While in high school, I was only seen as part of a group and never stood out as myself. I was considered "one of the AVID students" and only ever that. But, here I am a student leader one that wants to use his emotional skills to guide students, one that will help them overcome their troubles, one that will pick them up when they are down because I know. I have become Vice-President of the Everyone is Our Priority Club. Here I have overcome my fear of not feeling accepted. It is here that I am growing into who I want to be in the future.

What does the future hold for me? I cannot say for sure. I do not know how events will unfold and I do not know what challenges I will face. However, I can say what I hope to accomplish. I want to graduate from CSU Channel Islands with a Bachelor's of Science in Health Science with a minor in Psychology by Spring 2019. After I want to head straight to Graduate School at either University of San Diego or Western University of Health Science and be enrolled in their MEPN (Masters Entry Program in Nursing) so that I can be able to become a Nurse Practitioner in either Family or Pediatrics. With this job, I will use its high paying salary to first pay off my student loans and after take care of my mother.

Throughout my life, two people have been with me from the start; they are the ones that have been dealing with the same problems. My mom and my sister have always helped me and gave up life and happiness for me. They have done so much for me that even though I am aware that I will never repay them for everything they have done, I want to do everything I can to make their life easier.

    In my life, I have made many mistakes. I have had many failures. I faced a lot of stress and challenges when I was younger, I wish I had not faced. But I am okay with this. With every obstacle, problem, and failure I went through it was for the better. Every part of my life has made me into the person I am today. It is this negativity that I will turn into a positive. I will turn my weakness into my strength. No matter what obstacle I face or what path I go on, I will continue to move forward.

ANGELINA

I am a junior standing college student at CSUCI. I was born in Lazaro Cardenas, Michoacán, Mexico. I was brought into the United States when I was two months out of the womb. I was brought in illegally, through border patrol inspection where I passed in as another baby. I grew up in Riverside, part of the Southern Californian culture. Thankfully, I've been able to experience multiple cultures in the aspect of my Spanish-speaking home and the diverse population in my surrounding community.

Always knowing my legal status and limitations, I never was a student with ambitious goals. In high school, all my peers were planning which universities they'd go off to while I was just nonchalantly going through school. I was fortunate to have such a motivating counselor who did not allow me to settle for community colleges. Thanks to her, I am now attending CSU Channel Islands and in the Educational Opportunity Program where I have grown so much in as a student and as an individual.

I've joined student organizations, clubs, and even gotten involved in chair positions. I was also motivated to work for EOP as a Student Assistant at their center and even experienced their Summer Bridge transitional program twice - once as an incoming student, and the second time as a peer mentor. All this involvement has given me the opportunity to grow as an individual with a broader interdisciplinary point of view. This also kept me distracted from the whole undocumented part of my life until this past summer.

This past summer, my grandmother grew overwhelmingly sick. During this time, I was hearing about Advanced Parole, a permission for re-entry into the United States due to a special circumstance where the recipient must leave to their country. It was specifically through DACA (Deferred Action for Childhood Arrivals). We knew my abuela was heading to her final days so I went to Homeland Security and asked for this emergency travel to meet the lady I spoke to through the phone while growing up - the lady I was named after - before it was too late. My documented aunt had to drive me to the office instead of my mother who feared of the worst. I was prompted to a short angry brown-skinned Asian as the immigration officer reviewing my case. I think he hates nopales because he didn't check all my documents before sending me away to different places three times in a row. This needs to be translated (because Spanish was not a job requirement), this has to be officially stamped (just wasting your time), you need to get your fingerprints scanned though you just did a couple months ago (I don't like you, nopal). My grandmother no longer wanted to talk on the phone and the day before I had my appointment to complete all the documents for reviewing, she passed away.

"What's the point of going now anyway? She's already dead" the nopal hater said and then waited for a response from me before another officer handed him my approved and signed letter from their supervisor.

I didn't, and still don't, understand why he was so cruel. Because of him, I was not able to see my abuela alive, but dead. Getting buried in the ground next to my abuelo, my heartache only grew towards anger. This is how I was treated; I couldn't imagine what they've done to others.

I was able to re-enter the US legally with the letter. Probably because of this, if I later apply for citizenship, I would not have to be sent out to Juarez, Mexico, to see whether or not I'd get pardoned for my illegal entry. I've only heard about how it could take over a decade before hearing a response from USCIS. My mother said that my abuela's death was a miracle in disguise for my situation.

    Summer ended and the US elections were approaching. Surprisingly then, Trump was still in the running against Hillary. Not a lot of people thought he would make it too far. His supporters rising in all states made me and everyone around me uncomfortable. Then one night, my boyfriend of five years asked me to marry him for fear that our love might be severed through deportation. I saw in him the fear that my eyes had at the immigration office. My parents quickly agreed while his parents were more hesitant.
We got married in August. Trump won in November that same month we sent in all the documentations we needed for me to apply for US citizenship.

Marriage was not something I wanted to do before finishing school, but I did it because I might not have had the option if we waited. I wanted to marry my love, but I was not ready to. He was not ready either. I didn't want to get married this way. I didn't want us to get married this way. I didn't want to apply for citizenship. I didn't want to apply to be a citizen in the only country I have ever lived. Why do I have to? I've lived here my entire life. This is the only land I've been stepping on, the only place where the wind has picked up my breath. The culture my parents created is at my house, here. I went to public school my entire life here. My parents said farewell to Mexico without turning back while both their mothers were dying. They've jumped from job to job, speaking little English, hoping E-Verify wouldn't step on their new employment. My parents became the strongest individuals I've ever known because they've stayed to keep me and my little sister here, in this land of opportunity. So, I did it.

Last week, my husband received a letter from USCIS: it's our appointment. They scheduled it for a month from now. The week right after finals week (mid-May, 2017). We'll have to go in with additional documents and proof of our marriage being done in good faith. I'm not worried about it because I still have that anger inside of me built from the summer that dares them. I don't know what will happen, but I'm not afraid. I know many are, though they shouldn't be. What's the worst that can happen? Probably not being kicked out, but being stuck in this country's oppression.

We need to educate and share stories to others who may be going through the same experience. It's so easy to feel alone, but that's what their plan is, to make you feel alone, like an alien to this country. I want to advocate and share what I've learned to aide others. Their stories may not be the same as mine, but hearing what some have gone through creates a safer ground. Though it's not in my career path, I do want to form an outreach to other DREAMERs, to other undocumented peers. Creating safe places and a support system that allows for expressions to be known. Right now I am just a junior-standing student at CSUCI, but I'm forming connections here and there, spreading my voice, spreading my story.

MADDISON

As a child, I didn't get to experience the type of mother and daughter relationship that most girls get to have with their mothers. Often, my mother had lots of company. It seemed that there were always people I didn't know coming in, or going out of our house. I felt like a stranger in my own home. Because my mother lived such an unstable life, I often lived with my grandmother.

There were many nights when I was living with my grandmother that I waited for my mother to call. She would tell me she was coming to spend the night with me. I would stay awake as long as I could, waiting. When I could no longer keep my eyes open, I would fall asleep with the hope that when I awoke the next morning my mother would be there, lying beside me. Many nights she disappointed me and attempted to make it up to me by bringing me candy or a toy when she came to visit. My mother was addicted to drugs and that is why we couldn't have the type of relationship I always longed for.

My mother's addiction to drugs caused me to learn to be self-sufficient at a young age, because there were so many things she never taught me. She was preoccupied and neglectful. She wasn't the type of parent who was involved in activities or meetings at my school, and the few times she did show up, I was embarrassed at her disheveled appearance.

Consequently, my grandmother became a second mother to me. When I was almost taken away from my mother and placed into foster care, it was my grandmother who stepped in and took on the responsibility of raising me. It was difficult because she had to secure a babysitter for me while she went to work. She also struggled to help me with my homework when I needed it, so I had to find other resources to assist me. What she did was love me, by providing me with a safe place to live and making sure I did well in school. My grandmother also took me to church. In short, my grandmother's intervention into my life while my mother struggled with her addiction is what saved me.

    After my brother's death, I too was distraught, but I realized that I needed to be strong in order to help my mother. I was determined to be an even better student so that she could be proud of me. I knew that she felt hopeless and needed something to lift her spirits. Though I tried to fill the void of my brother, I was fighting a losing battle. Consequently, my mother and I drifted further apart. Recently, however, we have begun making monumental strides to mend our relationship.

After battling drug addiction for many years, my mother is now clean. I discovered that no longer am I that little girl wanting desperately to have the love of her mommy. Instead, I am a strong, courageous young lady who no longer feels incomplete. I realize that I am enough with or without my mother's love. Over time, we did gain that mother and daughter bond I always looked for. We also ended up getting closer than ever.

My future aspiration is to attend medical school to become a Nurse Practitioner and work in a Neo-Natal Intensive Care Unit. I love children, and I want to provide the love and nurturing that children need in order to get well and thrive. I realized when I was a child that my mother loved me, but I received love from her when she was capable of providing me with love, not consistently like I needed it. Growing up, I often felt vulnerable and lonely. This is why I want to work with seriously ill babies. They are the most vulnerable in society and in need of the most love and nurturing.

I am glad to say that I am very happy to be a part of the EOP program. Without the love and support from them, I don't think I would've been able to get through my first year of college.

TIMBER

I was born on December 12, 1996, in the City of Ho Chi Minh City, Vietnam. I spent the next nine years living with my mom at my grandma's house alongside eight other family members. Growing up in district 4 -considered the toughest district and most dangerous one in all seven located in the South- is still by far the hardest thing I had dealt with in my life. My mom worked three jobs just so that I could attend Elementary School, because the Vietnam school system costs a fortune. The majority of the kids grew up with zero knowledge and uneducated because most of them started working as kids. As a child, I knew that it would be impossible to get out of the "ghetto." Even as a kid, I felt oppressed by this system of communism. I remembered the phrase "the American dream" like it was a dream. Everybody lived their life wishing that one day, somehow, they would get an opportunity to leave Vietnam. In 2005, me and my mom had this opportunity thanks to my current step-father which I consider my real father. It was indeed a blessing; I was so happy that I could have my own "American dream." So, there I am on the plane flying to the United States, all I could really think about is how lucky I am to be the only kid in my family given this opportunity. The moment we landed I felt a huge relief like life will only get better from here on. It was quite the opposite at the beginning, my experience of culture shock was a little bit too much for me to handle. Elementary school hit me like a ton of bricks. For months, I had no friends because I knew little to no English. I stumbled numerous times before I eventually got comfortable with the American culture. Little by little, I gained more confidence in school and society, now I am the first in my family to attend college.

DEBBIE

When I was growing up, financial insecurities were a constant occurrence in my household; it wasn't until later in my life that I came realize that this was not the way most individuals lived. To me, helping my parents raise money for expenses and refraining from luxuries and costly necessities was the norm. Growing up in a household where both of my parents immigrated to the U.S and often struggled to maintain a stable income definitely had its challenges, but I wouldn't change a single thing. The challenges I faced as an English learner, daughter of immigrants and first generation college student made me the person I am today. The sleepless nights of studying and arduous work that I have put forward have all been more than worth it. The path I've trekked so far has been difficult and has demanded more than I thought I was able to give, but has been the most rewarding experience. I've learned more than I thought I was ever capable of learning, I've visited more places than I could have ever imagined and I've met the most colorful and delightful people along the way.

My pursuit of higher education has been a big part of this journey as well as a huge contributor to my personal growth. I never thought that I would be so privileged as to attend a four-year University especially one filled with individuals who are constantly building me up. Coming to CSU Channel Islands has been one of the best decisions I've made thus far and I know it is one that I will happily look back upon. It is communities like EOP that have made my experience here more meaningful and memorable. Being able to experience both the rigors and joys of college with individuals of similar backgrounds has been a great motivator over these past few years. Despite the lack of guidance in such an unknown territory it's comforting to know that there are individuals right beside me eager to help. I know that my journey is not over yet and that there are more challenges that I will need to overcome, but I am confident that the path of higher education will lead to greater opportunities and a fulfilling future. Although, I don't have everything figured out I am happy with how far I've come and content with the pleasant surprises life has thrown my way. I hope that one day I can empower others the way the communities of Channel Islands like EOP have empowered me. I am anxious and excited to continue to write the next chapters of my life. I am a first generation college student, a Latina, an English learner, daughter of immigrants, an ambitious dreamer, an eager learner, a girl with big dreams an open mind and a heart to help others.

DONNA

When I think back to my life I think I had a pretty great one. I have had multiple downs but have always somehow been able to bring myself back up. The best part is rising back a lot stronger than when I fell down in the first place. I grew up about two hours away from CSU Channel Islands in the city of Ontario. Growing up, I lived with my mom, my dad, my older sister, and my older brother. We lived in a two-bedroom house in a pretty sketchy neighborhood, but that place was my home. When my sister went to college we moved to a bigger house and a less sketchy neighborhood. While living here, I went through a lot. When I was younger my parents fought almost every night. It was in this house that they decided to separate for a while. My dad disappeared and only showed up when he promised. I was happy because I got to see my dad and all I wanted was for him to come back. I think my parents saw what the separation was doing to us so they got back together after about a year of separation. Not too long after that my mom started getting sick. She would go to the doctors and they said that she had asthma. They never did any real tests until it got really bad and we took her to the main branch of our hospital. They took some x-rays and told her that it could be a fungal infection or lung cancer. I remember that night before we had to leave her in the hospital; laying in the bed with her I said, "I hope you have fungus in your lungs." Sadly, it wasn't fungus. My mom had stage four lung cancer. It started in the lungs and began to spread to her brain. I was devastated.

They immediately began to give my mom radiation treatments for her brain tumors, because they were smaller than the lung tumors. She finished radiation treatment and her brain was cancer free. I was so excited. Then they went to the chemo. I didn't really know that chemo could be so hard on the body. I watched my mom go through a lot. When she was doing okay, she could stay home and do her chemo from there. One time she had to go to the restroom so I helped her walk there. My dad had just left to go to the store, so I helped her cause she couldn't hold it any longer. We got there, I helped her sit down, and she called me when she was done. I walked in and she couldn't get up. She couldn't stand and get off the toilet. Her legs were so weak and the toilet was so low that she couldn't do it. That was one of the first times I saw my mom cry when she was going through chemo. I tried to help her, but I was too weak. I told her I'd get my brother, but she wouldn't let me. She didn't want him to see her like this. So we waited for my dad to come. When he came, I told him and he ran to my mom and helped her up and held her while she cried. It honestly broke my heart having to watch all of this. Not too long after the toilet incident, my mom got really sick. I woke up one morning and heard a lot of noise. I stepped out and I saw my mom getting taken away by an ambulance. From then on, my mom stayed in the hospital. One day after school my brother and I went to the hospital. All my family was there and they asked us a question. They asked if we wanted our mom to come home because she was dying. I immediately said yes, but they wanted us to think about it. Before my brother and I could really answer, my mom past away. I was twelve when this all happened.

    My life after that was never really the same. I knew my dad really missed my mom and I knew that he was broken from her death. We spent a lot of time trying to get over the fact that she was gone. I feel like my dad sunk into some kind of depression; he had no drive. I would find him staring and crying at pictures of him and my mom. I always tried to be strong for my dad and my brother by not showing my emotions to them and by hiding when I would cry. I know now that doing that wasn't the wisest choice. I had a lot of pent up anger and rage that I didn't know how to express. So I got angry at my dad and my brother all the time. I yelled, threw tantrums and cried when they were sleeping. My life was on a rollercoaster after my mom passed away. When I turned sixteen, everything got a little better until we got evicted from our apartment. After that I moved in with my sister. I always thought my dad would come back for me and that my dad was going to get me and my brother back, but it never really happened. When I moved in with my sister, I was really able to cope with my mom's death. I truly accepted that my mom was gone when I was seventeen years old. I really have to thank my sister for helping me, because without her I wouldn't be where I am today. She was my savior during the darkest times of my life. She believed in me and pushed me to be the best I could be, someone that my mom would be proud of.

My sister and my mom were the driving force for me to go to college. When I first got here to CSU Channel Islands, it was amazing. I hit a really low point in my life when I thought that I wasn't going to make it through college. I was placed on academic probation after my second semester at CSUCI. I kept it from everyone I love, because I was so embarrassed and ashamed of myself. During the time on academic probation I met my boyfriend. He really gave me inspiration to get off and continue with school. I spent my whole second year at CSUCI on probation and being on probation was truly a life altering experience. My second semester on probation I took this performing arts class that really opened up my world. It helped me get over the resentment I had over my father and helped me connect with him once again. It showed me that my life wasn't tragic at all that I was lucky because my parents taught me how to live a life full of love.

Currently I believe I have really found my balance at school and in my own life. My freshman year and my summer of freshman year were a whirlwind. I am truly blessed to be in the place I am today, I am graduating this Summer 2017. The people that are in my life right now are the most amazing people in the world. They inspire me and truly help me when they don't even know they are doing it. My roommates, my boyfriend, his family and my family give me meaning. My goal, and the reason I continue going on, is to make all those people proud. I strive to succeed in all my classes and always try my hardest to do what is best for the people I love and also for me. Right now I am at peace. I still fight with the devils inside my head when times get rough, but I've learned not to listen to them. I believe that going to CSUCI was the best decision I have ever made in my whole life. It has shaped me to who I am today and it has helped me become the person I have always wanted to be.

  College has helped me in my life more ways than one. I see things in a much more positive light. I know that I will be able to make it through anything because this school and EOP has taught me I am the strongest person in the world. In the future, I see myself becoming extremely successful and not letting my past experiences rule me. My childhood and my teen years have built me to who I am today and I plan on not looking back and just moving forward. I will always have those memories of the past within my heart but my new experiences are mine to mold. I am excited and I truly anticipate what is to come in my life. I don't know exactly what that is just yet, but I know that something positive and meaningful is in my future.

EZRA

As a first generation, low-income and AB-540 college student there are many obstacles you have to confront as you try to navigate through college, with the hopes that one day you will accomplish your educational goals. I was born and raised in San Salvador, El Salvador. I come from a single parent household comprised of my mother, my older brother, and my two younger sisters. Throughout life, I have faced many challenges that have shaped me to be who I am today: a strong, independent, smart person.

My family and education are two of my main values. My mother serves as my inspiration to always strive for something better and do well at school. She has taught me that things in life may not be as we would like them to be, but we always have to try and make the best of them. My mother migrated to the United States when I was only nine years old, with the hopes of providing my siblings and I with a better future. Back in El Salvador, she saw no future for us due to much violence and the lack of resources. Unfortunately, she had to leave my siblings and I behind. That was one the most difficult decisions she has ever made, but in the end it was all worth it. Five years after she migrated, she brought my siblings and I here to the United States. At first, I had a hard time trying to adapt to the new environment, new culture, and the people. What I struggled the most with, and still continue to struggle a little bit, is with the English language. Even though I had a difficult time at school because of the new language, I was still doing well academically in high school.

In high school, I met many wonderful people that supported me through my journey. Unfortunately, the roads in my journey were not always filled with roses, but with thorns and obstacles as well. When I was in high school, I experienced discrimination and racism. Many times I was made fun of because I did not know how to speak English and I was discriminated against for not being born here. All those negative experiences, instead of bringing me down, served to motivate me to learn English even faster and to excel at school. Perusing a higher education became one of my goals, but it seemed that I would not have any chances since none of my family members had attended college. Also, I was behind with my English and I did not have that many resources or guidance on how to apply to college. It was not until I applied to a program named Migrant Education Program that I started to receive guidance and support. Through this program, I had the opportunity to visit different universities such as University of California, Santa Barbara, University of California, Santa Cruz, California State University, Monterey

Bay, and California State University, Long Beach. The program motivated and encouraged me to always peruse my dreams and to work hard for them.

After becoming part of the Migrant Education Program, I joined many clubs at school such as the Latinos Unidos Club and Red Cross Club that got me more involved in school and with the community. I also got to learn about Advanced Placement Classes that I started to take advantage of my junior year. In my senior year, I ended up taking five AP Classes that prepared me for college and that raised my GPA from a 3.5 to a 3.7. After working extremely hard in high school, completing all my GE requirements and graduating with honors, I decide to apply to college. Surprisingly, I got accepted into almost all the ones I applied to, including CSU Channel Islands (CSUCI). At first, I did not know where to go. When I found out that I had gotten into the Educational Opportunity Program

(EOP), it made my decision easier to make. Consequently, I decided to attend CSU Channel Islands.

Now that I am here at CSU Channel Islands, I feel very fortunate to be part of an amazing program that has done so much for me. The EOP program has offered me a new family, a support system both economically and emotionally. It has also made my transition from high school to college easier through a Summer Bridge Program in which I got to learn many things and meet amazing people. It has also made me feel that I do have a chance to accomplish my educational goal which is to become a counselor or a Spanish professor. I am currently double majoring in Spanish and Psychology, and I plan to obtain a translation certificate as well. I am involved with many clubs such as the EOP Club, Soccer Club, Spanish Club, and I.D.E.A.S Club. Soccer has always been part of my life, consequently, I am playing with the school soccer team. I also do community service with the non-profit organization FOOD Share in Oxnard, California. I recently I got accepted to the Summer Undergraduate Research Fellowship program here at CI and likewise, was inducted into the Sigma Delta Pi Alpha Alpha Omicron Honor Society.

I, who was first was made fun of for not being born here and for not knowing how to speak English, have been recognized by the Senate as well as the Assembly of California for my academic excellence and commitment towards achieving my goals. Each of my achievements would not be possible without the support from my family, programs such as the EOP program, and friends who are always here for me. What I want to do in the future is to inspire low-income, AB-540, and first generation college students like me to follow their dreams. There has been, and there still are many situations, that are trying to stop me from accomplishing my dreams, but I know that the struggle I am in today is developing my strength for my future. In life we will always have to face many struggles, but as Christian D. Larson says "Believe in yourself and all that you are. Know that there is something inside you that is greater than any obstacle."

LILIAN

This is me. Determination to me is staying strong, being resilient, and fighting for what you want no matter how rigorous or crucial circumstances can be. I was born into a society where your character is defined by race, class ranks, or generation. These stereotypes that surround me complicate my life, making my aspirations and societies expectations difficult to reach. Despite these setbacks and the perceptions about where I come from, I am not a negative statistic and I continue to be persistent reaching success. I come from a broken home, a poor family, living in an impoverished community where many become a product of their own environment. I was raised by my mother a single parent of eight children, me being the youngest as well as the first to aim for a University education. Growing up I had the opportunity to admire my mother's strong structure, her devotion to keep me and my siblings alive and well. My hardships began at a very young age when my father left me and never came back. This has always brought disturbance to my life and an unexplainable sorrow that has haunted me. I have always waited for the day where I would receive a letter or a call explaining his absence, but all that has provided me is disappointment. He abandoned me like I was nothing leaving me to feel worthless; I could never understand how a man could just walk out on his family. I didn't know much about him but I always pictured him as a weak, coward who couldn't carry his own weight. My mom, on the other hand, has never left my side; she is and always will be the hero that lit the fire for me to carry down my road towards success. She gave me not only the strength to conquer all the hardships and obstacles life brought me, but also the love that brought my aspirations to life. She never gave up always putting a roof over my head, food on the table, and never walked out on me no matter how hard life got for her. My life begins here overcoming the struggle to cope with life's obstacles. Regardless of pain and sorrow, failure is not an option for me. I feel that during those times I walked amongst the darkness with a smile on my face, illuminating my own light creating determination in my heart. Each struggle I have encountered whether I failed or succeeded provided a life lesson, many of which come from people I have met along the way. Many people who have crossed my path believed they were better than me, because of where I come from. I used this negative aspect that these people provided to motivate me, proving I was no less than any of them. As a result, my determination in school showed; I have always excelled in my courses. I have always viewed school as a privilege. My education is my most valuable asset and the key to the gateways of success. I have always known that if I have the knowledge, I will have the power to conquer all my fears of failure and reach the success I truly want.

    My mom didn't make a lot of money so we were constantly on the move. As a result, I moved from school to school throughout my life. Even though this made me fall behind in school work, I never got discouraged. I just kept going and kept striving to do my best. School work and projects were really hard for me, because I never had the proper resources like other kids had. However, that never stopped me from getting a good grade. I always managed to use the resources around me.

    After living struggle after struggle, I promised myself even through the toughest times I would pull through it and make it out. I take pride in the scars hardships have left upon me, they remind me of the struggles I overcame throughout my life. Every scar has a story. Every journey has a path. My path was illuminated by blood, sweat, and tears. The hardships and obstacles of life molded me into a person who is thirsty for knowledge, as well as knitting my soul with faith and hope. I didn't have a million dollars or an enormous mansion; I only had an education to make me feel equal to others. Then there was a time when my life came to a crashing halt. Overwhelmed with life's challenges, I started to give up. I felt defeated like a failure who couldn't reach her goals, and my dreams were constantly blurred by the living nightmares. I didn't think I could save myself from the drowning sorrows that filled my heart. However, I picked myself up finding resilience by observing my surroundings. I continued on the path towards success pulling life's weights along with me. I knew I could achieve because I believed I could do anything as long as I put my mind to it, as well as the ever burning passion behind it.

  Today as obstacles approach me, I am equipped to handle them with an optimistic attitude. In all honesty, I appreciate the hardships life brings me; they've made me stronger and wiser as a person having to live through them. My setbacks got me ready for life's biggest achievement, failure was the cousin to success for me. Today I prove all those judgmental people wrong, and show them that it doesn't matter where you come from or what ethnic group you are in. I've grown to be humble and realize success can be achieved as long as you are determined to reach it. Determination is the key factor in my life, making me persistent to be all that I can be. Determination has kept me going even through the most difficult times, I will always be successful and achieve my goals as long as I keep the mindset I have. I always remember it's not where you come from, it's where you are going that matters.

DREAM

Ironic, isn't it? The dreadful task it is having to describe yourself on paper. I mean, truly, what person knows you better than *you*? Correct me if I'm wrong, but there isn't anyone in this entire universe who has spent more time with your own, raw, beautiful self than *you*. And yet here I am. Blank. Utterly floating in my own stream of consciousness, trying to pinpoint an event that would be interesting enough to talk about. But you see, that's the thing! I am fortunate, and have always considered myself to have been privileged with a beautiful life. Unlike some, I have never expected pity, nor work towards it. As a matter of fact, the challenges I have endured throughout my upbringing have shaped me into the person I am today, and the adversities I continue to face as a first generation college student have only strengthened my will to succeed.

Obtaining a college education has never been the norm in my family. To be quite honest, I did not even know I wanted to attend a four-year university until my senior year in high school. Fortunately for me, my parents had always instilled in me the importance of receiving good grades. As a consequence, making the decision to attend college was not too far from reality -or so I thought. Everything had seemed to be sailing smoothly until I began to look into the costs of attending. I quickly became aware that undocumented people like me were not eligible to receive federal financial assistance. I was devastated. How could I have worked so diligently for something and not be able to have the luxury of having a shot at higher education? Was my legal status deemed unworthy of attending? Whatever the case was, I knew I had to work ten times harder to be able to attend. I looked into scholarships directed towards Dream Act students, and was fortunate enough to have received plenty. I applied for all the help I was able to get my hands on, this of which brings me to my next best thing after being accepted to various universities: EOP.

    I still remember the first time hearing Kari's voice. It was sweet and welcoming. Even despite the limited help for Dream Act students, she motivated me to not give up. I would call the EOP Center what seemed like every day to ask if my application had been read, and when the acceptances would be sent out. I wanted to be part of EOP so badly that when I was offered a position on the waitlist, I took it without hesitation. A few weeks later, Daisy called, again with a sweet and welcoming demeanor. She wanted to know if there was any circumstance that would prevent me from attending EOP Summer Bridge. Barely containing my excitement, I let her know that nothing would stop me from taking on that amazing opportunity. May 2016 seemed to be the longest month of the year. I was ecstatic to be able to take part in EOP, and I could no longer wait to participate in Summer Bridge. When June 16th finally arrived, I was nervous because I didn't know what to expect, but nonetheless, I was ready to take on new adventures.

      EOP Summer Bridge flew by, and before I knew it, it was move-in day. I'm not going to lie. The first couple of weeks living on campus were hell. I felt out of place. I had made plenty of friends, but the idea of being away from home tormented me. While others were celebrating the absence of any rules, I was stuck contemplating my place within the university. I wanted, more than anything, to be home. I called my mom often and explained what I felt. She didn't really know what to say because she had never experienced me being away. I'm sure the house was lonely without me too. Being the grounded woman she is, I knew things had hit an all-time low when she confessed to me that it was okay to come home. That wasn't my mother. She is the strongest person I know, and for her to say that it was to okay to give up was something unheard of. I know my absence really took a toll on her. At that point in my life, I had a very important decision to make. I would either leave everything I had worked for behind, and go home, or I would push through, and do what I knew best, sticking to, and accomplishing my goals. Eventually, my fears faded away, and the semester rolled by. Before I knew it, Christmas had arrived.

    I was anxious to see my final grades, but I knew I had pushed through, and gave it my all throughout the entire semester. Once I saw that I had done really well, I knew that not only was I worthy of achieving a degree, I was also kicking ass in doing so. After this, I knew that I was now ready to take on an additional role. By this time, I was offered a position within EOP as an application reader. I was excited to start, but most importantly I was excited to read what these kids were made of. Being an application reader has thus far been the most rewarding experience I have taken part in within the university. The resilience exemplified by these students is truly uncanny. I read so many stories that revealed the hope that still exists for this messed up world. Each and every one of the stories I read was different, but in the end, they all had a common goal: coming to a four-year institution, and succeeding in order to someday be able to walk the stage. Being in EOP has allowed me to take part, as well as help others take part in something greater than ourselves. We are the gifted few who have been deprived of many tools for success, and yet here we are, and here we are to stay.

As humans, we crave belonging. It is in our instincts to want to be part of something. When a group works together towards a common goal, great things are accomplished. Being an active member of the EOP family has allowed me to acquire a strong sense of belonging within Channel Islands. If nothing else, I am an EOP student. That will remain with me wherever I go, and I know that I have plenty of individuals to thank for my continued success in college. There is no doubt that being a member has allowed me to step out of my comfort zone. I am no longer the first-year student terrified of the oblivion that comes with being the first in your family to attend college. I have learned to accept that nothing in life gets handed to you. Instead it is up to you to get yourself where you want to be. In the next few years, and with the support of my family, friends, and my "home away from home," I look forward to graduating, and obtaining my Bachelors of Science in Nursing. "Aquí estamos y no nos vamos!"

MARISOL

"Si se puede." Almost two decades ago, I was brought into a world where this was not only looked upon as our family's favorite motto but also as an ideal world filled with love, happiness, and encouragement for perseverance. As a child of immigrants who only spoke Spanish, required me not just to translate when others could not understand them but to constantly stay alert of those who tried to take advantage of them. Although they somehow managed to completely rebuild their lives after arriving to the United States and still provide for us, I always found them telling my brother and I how much "more" they wished they could have provided. However, looking back on my childhood, I have no complaints. I grew up in a world filled with opportunities for academic growth, unlimited support, spiritual guidance, and free from any worries. Nevertheless, who would have known that this state of innocence would soon come to an end the summer prior to my junior year in high school.

As my father's illness worsened, he became extremely incapacitated and depended on my family and I a majority of the time. When my mother and brother worked, I would wake up every morning and check on him, only to realize he had been lying in bed waiting for me to peek in. I would then make him breakfast knowing I'd have to beg for him to finish every bite due to his loss of appetite. In the hospital, my mom and I would take turns cutting his food, feeding him, helping him to and from the restroom, in and out of bed, giving him his oral medication, and having some of our last but endless conversations. I was touched by his pain when his frustration showed getting in and out of bed; I hurt when I saw his embarrassment after people staring at his bald and pale head; saw the struggles of his twig- like legs holding up his 6'1" frame, and will never encounter a deeper pain than when the doctor announced he had less than three months to live. Having him turn towards me, nod his head, and slowly turn away with tears in his eyes. As I saw his fear, it slowly lingered into my heart as well. Having all this to deal with, I still could not forget about my main priority: school. Since elementary school, time management has always been a necessity. My entire life I have lived in Oxnard but attended school elsewhere. My life routine, up until college, had always been to awake by 5AM, leave to Carpentaria by 6AM, and then return home by 4PM. However, between this, I still managed to receive straight A report cards, academic awards, and enroll in honors/AP/dual enrollment courses. Although it was then when it felt as if my world was beginning to fall, I looked at my father and knew that if I gave up now, my fighting would have been for nothing. Somehow throughout this experience, I found the strength to pull myself up and continue my path of "academic excellence," as the awards always said. I found the time to do my work, challenge myself, join clubs, and volunteer. Towards the end of his last days, I will never forget the moment he grabbed my arm and said, "No sabes lo tanto que estoy orgulloso de ti." Thinking back, I like to believe he never admitted just how proud he really was because he saw how much effort I put into everything. Now having heard this from him, makes me the person I am today.

    I am a focused, determined, self-motivated, and diligent. I am the person who will continue pushing herself through college, the nursing program, and any future goals because I know that my future would have made my father proud. From the moment my father told me about his cancer diagnosis, I was forced to face challenges and emotions most 16 year olds would never be forced to confront. The death of my father forced my sense of responsibility, religious belief, and view on the world to take a drastic turn. However, if it would not have been for me taking care of him, volunteering, joining clubs, challenging myself, and having gone through what I have, I would not have realized the career choice which is ideal for me: someone who helps others, a nurse. Today, however, I have begun to view the world much more realistically; a dream is merely that if no action is taken. Amidst all the excitement that came with successfully completing my first college semester and almost year, I've not only learned that self-responsibility is key, but also that one must be willing to push themselves through the fear/self-doubt that comes alongside being a first generation college student. Adjusting to a new college culture may be difficult, but in order to grow as a student and eventually adapt, one must not only learn from their mistakes, but also embrace newly taught information, techniques, and skills to reach their goal and excel through college.   After having made the decision to enroll in CSU Channel Islands, I began looking further into CSUCI's Nursing Program prerequisites and requirements. Currently, I have completed two and will begin the application process to various Nursing Programs in December 2017, after having completed the remaining three courses. Moreover, depending on the particular program, it will take me anywhere between 2-3 years to successfully obtain my BSN degree.

      Aside from having those academic plans, I will also remain actively involved in clubs within CSUCI and outside organizations. Since December 2016, I've been volunteering with a program called

COPE Health Scholars. This program is not only partnered with UCLA's Fielding School of Public Health, but was also said by our department coordinator, Sarah Contreras, to have been an internship program designed for college students pursuing a career in the medical field. Within the program, a Health Scholar's scope of practice is very similar to that of a CNA's. We have been given the opportunity to work beside nurses and physicians at St. John's Medical Centers to gain clinical experience as well as provide basic care for patients. Just like I had previously done with my father, I am expected to help feed, bath/cloth, transport, and change patients. Then as I accumulate volunteer hours, I will have the option of working within additional hospital departments that offer far more duties/opportunities. I am beyond grateful for having been accepted into this program as it will not only offer me actual hands on experience, but also expose me to a much bigger variety of health care professions that may spark an interest or influence me to pursue a career path that I had not yet considered.

My father passed on August 12, 2013. However, this experience has made me realize just how much I love challenging myself, working towards a better life, and helping others. It was an experience that will forever keep me grateful of all the opportunities, people, and things that I have come across in my life. As summer approaches, I plan on using my vacation time wisely. Not only do I plan on taking summer courses, but also find a part time job which will allow me to save money and continue helping my family financially. Additionally, I will continue to work toward completing the 280 hours required by COPE before successfully graduating from the program. Lastly, I will continue to grow academically, expand my knowledge, and make the time to help others in the community. I plan on succeeding not only for myself, but also for my father and the many who have helped support me mentally as well as financially up to this point. I will continue to transcend any hardships, cherish every opportunity given to me, and be grateful for the support system that continuously encourages me to reach for the stars. Going to college, bettering my education, remaining an honor roll student, becoming independent, getting my medical license, having a stable job, and knowing one day I will be financially secured is something that I've always wanted for myself. So, as I continue on this journey, I will take this experience and mold it into motivation. Whenever I feel I am in a situation I can no longer get past, I'll remind myself that if my father never gave up fighting for his life, I have no right to give up fighting for anything less meaningful. I will never give up fighting for anything I have my mind set to.

"Si se puede."

CHRISTOPHER

February 17, 1996, I was born. Now I don't have a great story of how I was born in a field, or in a barn, or at home. I was born in a hospital in Oceanside, California, to my mother and my father. Let's fast-forward a couple years to elementary school. We lived in Lancaster in a semi-okay neighborhood, but still a ghetto with gangs and drugs. It was me, my mother and my little brother Robert. My dad wasn't around; he was in jail for a while, but when he was out he would only send me things. I never had his presence. While I was in elementary school my family and I moved around a lot. We went from a house to different apartments, then for some time we lived in our green van. I loved this van because it would possibly be mine one day, then it would have been my very first car. Even though it wasn't, I still remember everything about the van from the forest green paint job to the ripped seats that had a claw like design in the rear seat. My mother always gave us the best she could and even though we didn't have much, everything I did have meant the world to me. I didn't fully understand what being poor was until I would go on field trips with my class. The other kids had money to buy lunch and would spend money on food and at the gift shops buying souvenirs. All I had was a PB&J and a bag of hot fries and a couple bucks to buy a drink. But even though I was poor it never really bothered me much.

Yeah I did wish I could have all the things other kids had, but what kid didn't want that? At a very young age I had to learn how money works. My all-time favorite phrase my mom would say is "money don't grow on trees," and I always thought she was silly to say that. I soon learned what she was trying to tell me. We always had enough to get by and I remember we would go to food giveaway and there were these knock-off hot fries that we would get that me and my brother loved. We would rummage through the free groceries until we found the good stuff. We didn't always have to go to the giveaways only when times were the toughest which in some case was all the time. But as long as my brother and I were happy, my mother was too. Me and my brother didn't always get along. Since he was only a year younger than me, he still felt like he could tell me what to do even though I was the big brother. We did fight a lot growing up, but now we are closer than before. Even though he is still stubborn as hell, I love him. I'm the only one that can hit him; if anyone else did, then they would have to deal with me. My brother understood this very well and so did everyone else.

As a kid, just like learning how money is handled, I also learned how to pay bills by about six or seven. I would go into the Edison store front, or wherever we could pay our bills, and my mother would give me the money and would always tell me to get a receipt. With these skills instilled in me at a very young age, I matured very fast. I learned how to save money and I learned how to make money. I still remember my first job helping this guy sell burned CDS, on the corner of our liquor store, down the street from my house. He would send me to talk to all the adults, because he knew they were more likely to buy from a kid. I learned very quickly how to appeal to people's emotions in order to get them to do what I wanted them to, or to get the reaction from them that I wanted.

When I got to high school, this is where my life took a turn into the most difficult storm of my life, emotionally and physically. Actually starting in middle school is when my mother's medical problems became more severe, year after year. The most dramatic was my sophomore year of high school. On September 5, 2015, my mother, brother, stepfather at the time and I decided to go to a party hosted by one of my mom's childhood friends. We all decided to go to this backyard, BBQ, pool party and we were there all day. Finally, we decided to leave because my mom's oxygen tank was running low and she was having pain in her feet, because she is diabetic. The pain was so bad she decided to go to the hospital first thing in the morning. Normally I always go with her and at times I would miss school. However, I had good grades so I never suffered from missing classes. This was the first time I didn't go to the hospital with my mom, because I was up all night with her helping take care of her with my step dad. Her and my little brother, Robert, went and they were back before I woke up. She walked in gave me a kiss and I woke up to her kissing my cheek, telling me: "I'm back, baby. I'ma go lay down because I'm tired. I love you." I told her, "I love you too." It's now September 6, 2015, her brother's birthday and he comes over to celebrate with her. I've never been woken up to such distraught screaming in my life. My mom's brother went into my mom's room to wake her up- it's now about noon- and my mother is lying in her bed on her back; her face is purple, swollen and her tongue is sticking out.

    After hearing him scream her name, I jumped up off the couch- where I was sleeping next to my little cousin- and rush into the room to find my mother lying there dead. My mom's brother calls the ambulance, while we're there trying to get her out of the bed and onto the floor to perform CPR. We have a spoon down her throat to open her airways. The ambulance gets there within three minutes and I'm standing over my mom in shock, not knowing what to do, and my mom's brother and mother are trying to get me outside so I don't see. I refuse to leave my mother's side. I see them cut her shirt open and bring out the paddles. My mom's brother, Tony, pulls me outside and I snap. I'm so enraged with anger and hate towards god for taking my mother from me that I start punching my cousin's car, who was in the driveway, and denting his trunk while the medics carried my mother out on a stretcher. The medics managed to revive her, but her pulse was faint. They rushed her to the hospital. My mom was in a coma for a full year and had to have a trachea put in to help her breathe, and was heavily sedated so all I could do was talk to her and hope she could hear me. Every day, after school, I was there waiting with her even if I had to walk which the hospital was about 10 miles from my school. I would stay the night with her. I had so many visitor stickers that my bed frame was full of them. After multiple surgeries and six months of physical therapy, my mother was finally able to come back home. However, she wasn't the same. When my mother first woke up, she didn't remember who I was. I would say that hurt me more than watching her limp, dying body being carried out of the house. How could she forget her first-born son? Thankfully, she did remember me after some time; her memories finally came back to her. She never told me she didn't remember me, until about a year later, but I could tell by the way she looked at me when she first woke up she didn't know who I was. During the year my mother was in the hospital, my brother and I lived with our grandmother, Nana. During that time, she cared for us the best she could.

During my senior year of high school, when I was finally about to graduate, my mom was back home. At this time, my mom used a walker and was on 24/7 oxygen assistance because her lungs were too weak to breathe on their own. I would help my mother shower use the restroom and change clothes. To this day, I help her with some of these things, but she is now able to do most of them on her own. My senior year of high school I got accepted to three colleges: our local community college, California State University, Northridge (CSUN) and California State University Channel Islands (CSUCI). I was accepted into both EOP programs at CSUN and CSUCI, but my mother didn't want me to leave. I was ready to give-up going to a university and just go to our community college to be with my mother, because she meant the world to me. I had a dream that when I left, my mother was going to die again and this time she wouldn't be coming back. Losing my mother was my biggest fear. Thankfully my high school counselors, Mrs. Real and Mrs. Hale, were able to convince my mom to let me leave. They argued that going to college would not only better me as a person but our family as a whole. I decide to go to CSUCI and that would be my new home for my undergraduate, college career.

  My first day of school was my mother's first day back in the hospital. It felt as if my worst nightmare was starting to unfold. My mother was diagnosed with a collapsed lung, because she had fallen in the bathroom the night before I left to go to school. My entire first year of college my mom was in the hospital. And then, it happened. She died.

  I got a call one morning from my Nana and she was sobbing. I've only heard or seen her cry once: the first time my mother died. She sobbed:

"Colvy the doctors say she gone." My mother was infected with a virus that contaminated her blood. This virus you can only get from being treated inside a hospital. This was the second time the doctors tried to take my mother from me. After talking to my Nana, I jumped out of bed crying. I called my grandma, Grace, my dad's mom, and told her what happened and how my Nana said she's heading to the hospital to see what's going on. After talking to my grandma for about two hours, my NANA called me back saying they revived her and her heart is beating fine. She told me she's getting better and all her symptoms were going away. This was the day I truly knew there was a god because for my mother to die a total of three times in her life and come back every time, there could only be a god controlling these outcomes. I'll never forget all the wishes for her to "rest in peace" I've seen on my mother's Facebook page that day. After being released from the hospital again, and going through another six months of physical therapy, my mother finally came home the day before I finished my second semester of college.

    To this day, I'll never forget all the events I have been through to get me to where I am now. All the support I received from EOP, my friends, and my family helped get me through. I'm glad to say that my mother is finally home doing better than ever. I'm still going to CSUCI and working a fulltime job while being a fulltime student, and I talk to my mother every weekend driving home from work. The journey I have had to overcome has molded my mindset. Every time I think about quitting and wanting to give up, I think about all I've been through and how I got here. I use that to fuel me to finish what I start, so I can give myself and my entire family a better life.

The various events around my mother's illness in addition to my humble upbringing, have shaped and molded me into the person I am today. That's why no matter who I come across, I always try to be that positive person in their life. We have so much negativity and so much going against us, I want to be that person you can go to. I truly care about people and respect people, because we all come from different walks of life but we are all want the same out of life. It's the journey that can brings us together. I live by the motto: *the only thing stopping me from accomplish all my goals is myself*. I've come this far and I plan to go a lot further.

EOP Alumni from California State University Channel Islands wrote the following stories.

JUAN

In the year 2010 with a suitcase rolling behind me and tears in my eyes, we departed from what I once called home. La Barranca, a small town in Michoacán, Mexico, just outside of Mexico City, saw me be born and grow up and up until my preteens, it was the only world I knew. La Barranca gave me some of the best years of my life because I was young and had no worries. I lived with my mom, sister, and little brother. Unfortunately, I didn't get to see my dad much because he spent 11 months of the year working here in the United States, so that we could have a better life. Although I was sad to say goodbye to my friends and family, down deep I was happy because I was finally going to be able to see my dad every day. We made it to Juarez where we were given our visas and were granted permission to come to the United States. The United States was what I expected and much more. Here everything was straight, smooth with no flaws and things just seemed to flow smoother. I can admit that I was culture shocked because I wasn't used to the weird foods, the new language and a bunch of new set of rules to follow. School for me was only difficult in the beginning. The first day of class I tried speaking Spanish to a girl who did not answer my questions. Later that day, I found out that she only spoke English. I was so naïve because I was taken out of a small town in Mexico and placed in a completely different environment. I seriously thought people spoke Spanish and nothing else, and that everyone in the world spoke it. I also thought everyone liked the same things I did and celebrated the same things as my family. Within a year, I was speaking the English language with little difficulties. I along with my best friend, who migrated to the US the year before me, were the top students in my fourth grade class.

Everything started to change not long after we settled down. My mom and dad started working from 6:00AM to 7:00PM, and I didn't get to see them much. By the time they got home at night, I was already either in bed or fast asleep. I remember waking up when they walked in because the door to the room made a lot of noise. We couldn't afford to rent our own house so we were staying at my dad's brother's house. My family and I lived in a small little room where we slept on two old mattresses. You would think that because we were family we were treated fairly, but it was just the opposite. My aunt made our lives a living nightmare. She took our food, charged us outrageous prices for rent, scared us with the police if we didn't listen to her and woke us all up at 5AM. She harassed us as much as she wanted because she knew we had nowhere else to go. After six months of living there my dad had enough, so we saved up enough money to rent our own home and we moved out. To keep paying for rent and food my parents started working even more than they already were. I seriously felt like I raised myself for a long time. I missed them, but there was nothing I could do about it. They were forced to work long hours just to pay the bills and rent. After a few years of living like this, I began to think that leaving La Barranca, Mexico, had been a big mistake.

At age twelve I got tired of seeing my parents working so hard, while I did nothing at home. I convinced my parents to take me to work with them every school break from that point forward. The work was tough and I could see my mom didn't want me going, but I felt a sense of pride from my dad that I hadn't seen before. Every day we woke up at 5AM, and left to the lemon fields where we would start working from 6AM to 6PM. This was an adventure for me and I would not have traded that experience for all the money in the world. I remember the hot, blistering sun by midday, and the weight of the sixty-pound bag I carried around to pick the lemons. To me this wasn't difficult because I was with my parents all day for once in my life I was actually spending time with them. Every spring, summer and winter break I worked with them and I was ecstatic every time a break was coming. While most of my friends were out playing, I was in the fields working with my parents. My favorite part was when we had our break and we sat down for lunch, because it was like having a picnic every single day.

When I was about fifteen, things started to change. My dad started drinking more than what he was used to drinking perhaps it was because of all the stress he had. Because he didn't have a day to rest out of the week, I think it led him to alcohol to feel a sense of freedom. Our lives changed from that point forward. Because he was constantly drunk, he began to insult us which was a thing he had never done before. My dad went from a loving father to a mean unrecognizable man. At night, he would argue and fight with my mother and it was an everyday thing. He slammed doors, broke plates and threw things at us. We were living on constant abuse and harassment. That is when my grades went down, every night I had little sleep and I really didn't care anymore. I was tired of life, so I didn't do any assignments and I fell asleep in class all the time. Somehow I was able to make it through high school and I made it into college, but I did lose my relationship with my father. We spoke little. He wasn't a bad father, at least not when he wasn't drinking. He was a good man and to this day I remember him when we did spend time together.

Sadly, my father passed away summer of 2013, just before starting my senior year in college, and it was the most painful thing I had to endure.

After being arrested for what the police said was a DUI, although my mother denies that my father was drinking at the time, he was taken to jail. He was taken into custody and he never got back home, next morning a police officer came to our house to inform us that my father was in the hospital. We rushed there to find out that he had suffered from a stroke; we spent two days in the hospital before he passed but I never again had the chance to tell him that I loved him or even say goodbye. It's painful to remember that we didn't have a good relationship, and even more sad to know that I didn't hug him for years until he was dead in a hospital bed. Although this was a painful time in my life, I was able to complete my degree in four years. I graduated from CSUCI with a business degree. Even though he never told me, many of my dad's friends told me that he was really proud of me. They said that he would always tell them that his son was at a university and that he couldn't wait for me to graduate. Knowing this at the time, it fueled my determination more than ever to finish school for him and in his memory.

All my plans and goals for the future are not clearly defined yet. I do have one thing I want to do before I die. I want to create a non-profit organization that focuses on helping Hispanic immigrants living in the United States. My father's demise was alcoholism and it was the stress of working so hard that drove him to it; it drove him to lose himself completely and to lose the relationship he once had with his family. I don't blame my father or hold a grudge against him, on the contrary. Thanks to him, I attended college and was given the opportunity to write to you about him. If he hadn't had such a hard life that drove me to keep moving forward, I might not have come to college to get my parents a better life. I came to college to get them a better life, and now he can't enjoy that which he worked so hard to get me. Holding grudges or having resentment is not in my nature. I remember my dad only as a caring, loving, charismatic man. I have promised myself that if I get the chance to help immigrants like my parents, I will do so no matter what it takes. That is my personal dream that I hope someday will come true.

XIMENA

As a young child, I had dreams of going to a four- year university but it always seemed too far of a reach. I did not always see a definitive future for me, both of my older siblings dropped out of high school, my parents were undocumented and I was homeless at the age of nine, along with my mother and my little sister. My mother had always struggled financially and I felt that if I told her that I wanted to go to college, I was going to add another financial burden to her.

I was nine years old when we lost our apartment. My mom, my little sister, and I were homeless. Sometimes we had to alternate staying at friends' houses. Other times we slept in the car, hoping we would not get caught and risk Child Services taking us away from our mother. We took ten minute showers in the public park showers. When my mom didn't have enough money for gas, we woke up at five in the morning to go to school in order to take the metro. We often didn't arrive at our destination of sleep until ten at night. All my life, my mother has struggled to afford food and rent, but it is her struggle that has motivated me to do well for myself. I strive to obtain a good career so I don't have to go through what we went through ever again.

My guidance in life is that no barrier is too big to stop me from what I want to achieve. Along the way, I have experienced hardships in my life when I wanted to quit, when I felt I wasn't good enough. However, my mom has taught me that even when I am on my knees I must still maintain my stability and work harder to get back up again. I go to school, stay out of trouble, and dedicate a vast part of my time to my community because it is what makes me feel like a leader. My motivation to do well in school comes from wanting to graduate, get a career, and motivate others to the same.

Being a little girl was hard. I wanted to be the one to tell her: "it'll be okay, mom. I'll take care of it." That's why I don't take my opportunities in life for granted. While kids at that age were worrying about what game to play, I was worrying about when my next meal was going to be and helping my mom get it for me. The specific event of feeling hunger, in my life, is what has made me stronger. I desire a future when I can provide a good home for my mother and sister- a future where they don't have to worry about financial issues.

A poem that I always keep in mind is "The Rose That Grew from Concrete," written by 2Pac Shakur, specifically the line: "proving nature's law is wrong, the rose learned to walk without having feet. Funny it seems, but by keeping its dream, it learned to breathe fresh air." It made me realize that I shouldn't sulk over my problems and create barriers for myself because of what I have been exposed to throughout my childhood. I want to be the first to tell my mother: "it will be okay. we have made it." I saw that smile on my mother's face on the day that I graduated. I knew then that I made her proud of all the hard work a single mother had to endure in order to have food on the table and a roof over our family's head. I may be just a young woman who had a dream to succeed, but I live by the everyday challenge to better myself and achieve.

    Given that my career choices would entail me to be an exceptional citizen in society, I would have to be aware of the choices I make. Your character is determined by the actions you choose to make and that ethic is what I have gained through the years of being a well- rounded individual. I am the role model for my younger sister along with other fellow students that I have mentored over the years. I was the first in my family to graduate high school and the first to attend a four- year university and the first to earn a bachelor's degree leading me to my career choice of becoming a lawyer.

Over the years, I have learned that my life purpose falls under volunteering and mentoring others. When I was in high school, I mentored cadets, Girl Scout troop members and other peers of mine. In college, I was a University Experience Associate which linked me to a University course of freshman students at Cal State Channel Islands. I am connected to the class to meet with the students biweekly in order to mentor, assist, and act as a liaison between the professor and the students. This is my form of purpose because viewing the downfalls of our youth in society many of whom are marginalized in what they feel they are capable of.

Due to my desire to help marginalized youth recognize their potential, I graduated with a major in political science and am pursuing my law degree in graduate school. I want to help my community through politics and become a civil rights lawyer. My main goal would be to help diminish crime rates and increase the attendance rates in my community's high school. As a young student in the LAUSD district for twelve years, I did not have the support system that I now have in the EOP program, programs such as these are what help the youth of society to become well rounded human beings in the future.

MICHELLE

I remember riding in the back of my uncle Glem's car and him saying, "one day you're going to be the president!" I was eight and his words didn't go in one ear and out the other. They just bounced off. My mother was going through radiation for breast cancer and my concern wasn't being president, it was waking up to her the next morning. Her biggest concern was me getting to bed early that night to make it to school well rested the next morning. That was always her concern, school and it only took twelve years for me to understand why. Six years after her radiation for breast cancer, my mom died from gastric cancer. It was the most difficult thing I may ever experience in my life. I look back now and wonder how I made it through. How I didn't get pregnant at 15, how I managed to get my sister through school, keep my dad motivated and make it through high school and into a university. Ninety-five percent of that was my mom stressing me all my life about dedicating myself to school, partaking in athletics and extracurricular activities. In the end, it was all my involvement that got me through the loss.

Somehow, magically, as mothers do, she got me to understand that higher education was my way out of hardship and my way out of being a Hispanic stereotype. She got me to comprehend that I wasn't meant to be a statistic. My mother was my home. In the time between losing her and being accepted into CSU Channel Islands, I was lost. I was lost about who I was meant to become, what career path I needed to follow and how I would even get there. When I walked onto campus and into the EOP Summer Bridge Program, suddenly I was back home. Why? Because EOP shared my mother's vision. They knew I wasn't meant to be a stereotype. They knew that, my psychological trauma put aside, my rough home environment put aside, my flaws put aside, and I was worth their investment. They gifted me faith, they gifted me opportunity and like my mom could have told you, I took it. As I've said, I credit ninety-five percent of my determination to succeed in school to my mother. The other five percent of the reason I succeeded is because EOP believed in a girl from Los Angeles who had nothing but a passion to be anything but a statistic. While attending CSU Channel Islands I was the student government president two consecutive years and the first EOP student to become president of the student body. I guess my uncle Glem was right. My uncle Glem planted a seed, my mom planted a seed, and I just needed a little water. EOP was willing to water my thirst for a better future and today, I have not fully bloomed. I'm in the process of blooming and along the way, I am collecting a little bit of water, so that one day I can be the faith and opportunity that helps a student like me bloom.

LILO

I like to compare my life to that of a caterpillar. I keep a quote framed by the side of my bed and it goes: "just when the caterpillar thought its world was over, it became a butterfly." It reminds of me of a time that was very dark in my life, but that, paradoxically, brought so much life and light into the person that I am now.

I was born on September 22, 1991, in Ventura, California. My birth was a miracle. My mother had been in labor for many hours and the doctor had told my dad that there was a strong possibility that one of us would not make it. Well, here I am and I am blessed to also have my beautiful mother here with me to share this journey called life. With this being said, I know I have a purpose. I continue to strive to find it and God willing, I will find and fulfill this purpose.

Both of my parents are from Zacapu, Michoacan, Mexico. I cannot even begin to explain how much I love being Mexican. Growing up in the United States has influenced many of my interests, but I have kept myself deeply rooted in my Mexican culture. I love our traditions, our food, our poetry, our literature, and although I am not a fan of *banda* music, I do love Spanish rock.

I am very lucky to call Sandra Baez my mother. She is the reason my childhood was so magical. She did everything she could to not have our family struggles affect me. I remember one night; our power was shut off. It was one of many difficult months for us and my mom was left to choose between paying the water bill or the electricity bill. Ironically, that night was one of the most memorable nights of my childhood. My mom got all of our bed sheets and made a fort over her bed. She grabbed a flashlight and we both lay under the sheets making shadow puppets. She told me all kinds of stories and I listened attentively, bright-eyed. I also remember going on afternoon walks around our neighborhood with my mom. We would count flowers and group them in colors. Every time we passed by my neighborhood preschool, I would look through the windows and tell my mom how badly I wanted to start "la escuelita." I was always a very curious child. I loved listening to stories, which is why I learned to read at a very young age. When all of the other children wanted to go to the puzzle or computer station, I stayed in the classroom library area, with my eyes glued to book after book.

When I was four years old, I asked Santa for a baby sister. I am not joking when I say that a year later on, December 25th of the year 1995, my younger sister, Maria, who we call Lilo because she looks like Lilo from *Lilo and Stitch,* was born. The doctors put a bright red Christmas bow on her head and I remember looking at her with so much love. My best friend was born. She and I have always been very close. We tell each other everything and she is like a part of me, I do not even want to think about her leaving to college; it makes my heart break into two. Overall, my childhood, in my eyes, was perfection. We were poor, but we were happy.

Middle school marks the beginning of the dark years. I was very different from all of the other kids. I noticed that everything was changing. My friends wanted to start having boyfriends and wearing make-up. I did not. This is when I stopped hanging out with many of the people I hung out with during elementary school. During this time, I had also begun putting on weight. My self-esteem hit the floor and I became unhealthily shy. I never wanted to go out. I remember crying myself to sleep until I saw the morning light coming into my window. I was also bullied. Not just at school, but by my own cousins at home. Believe me when I say, words cut deep. They really do. I believed what people told me and at the age of twelve, I began questioning why I was ever brought into such a painful existence. My life at home was not the greatest either. My father, although physically there, was never emotionally there for me. My mom was my rock, but she worked long hours every day. I was bullied constantly, to the point that I would fake being sick so that I did not have to go to school. When high school came around, I was terrified. Surely enough, it did not get better once I got there. I was not bullied anymore, but I was already damaged. All of the things others had already said to me were engraved in my heart. I was still overweight and I felt ugly and worthless. I know I have always been smart, but my grades would tell you otherwise. Junior year, I had an epiphany, an epiphany that saved my life. What if I could start over? What if I could leave those ghosts behind me and pretend that they had never, ever come to haunt my life? I thought, I could continue living my life the way I was now, letting other live for me. Or, I could change the direction of my life and prove to all of those who hurt me that I love myself too much to let them defeat my already tattered up, broken soul. So I was overweight, that's ok, I thought. I can change that! I was also not very social, but I knew that the solution would be to go somewhere new, somewhere where I could meet new people who did not know who the old me was. I wanted to go to a place where I could find myself, without those ghosts of the past: college.

    Fortunately, I still had time to turn things around. I began working really hard in school and I got really good grades. Through the help of AVID, my mommy, and my second mommy, my Tia Raquel, I set a goal to go to college. I must admit, I was scared. However, I had become stronger. I knew nothing worse than what I had experienced could happen.

Unfortunately, my second mommy and one of my best friends, my Tia Raquel, passed away my senior year of high school. It hit me really hard and I am only now starting to overcome the pain. She understood me like no one else did. She always reminded me how important it was to not let go of a dream. I knew getting into college would make her look down at me with a smile. I applied to CSUCI and got in. I was ecstatic! My journey at CSUCI was tremendously empowering. Once I started college, I began changing my eating habits and began taking spin classes almost every day. I lost 30 pounds and gained an incredible amount of confidence. With that confidence, came my courage to get out of my comfort zone and get involved in clubs and organizations. I also had the opportunity to go to Spain, which was a dream come true! I also got a job on campus as the EOP student assistant and that brought much joy to my heart. I surrounded myself with such powerful, kind souls each and every day. Students, who, like me, had struggled, but had a smile on their face and their head up high every day, ready to conquer each day's new challenges. The same year I became an EOP student assistant, I became an EOP peer mentor for EOP Summer Bridge. Me? Who would have thought the quiet, insecure girl in high school would ever take on a leadership role like this one? One in which my job was to guide, inspire, and mentor!

    Currently, my journey as an undergraduate student at CI reached its sunset. I am still making dreams come true as I go. I helped one of my professors with her Psychology research and had the opportunity to travel to another state, something I had never done before, to present at a psychology research conference! Also, the winter break before graduation, I traveled to another country where I always wanted to go: Japan. I am at a good place in my life, not perfect, but good. I have both of my parents with me, an adorable sister, my best friend, and my boyfriend. Honestly, I sometimes just want to jump around and yell with happiness. I cannot believe how good God is to me. Yes, I went through many tests, but I always managed to overcome! Now that I hold that degree in my hand, I remember walking the stage, looking out into the crowd, and blowing my beautiful parents a kiss. I do not know how I contained myself; so many emotions overcame me. I continue making them proud. Once my college journey was over, I began a new one. One day, I hope to hold a doctorate degree pursuing what I love, psychology. I want to help heal other souls because I know what it feels like to feel like you're broken. I was once a caterpillar, but I am now a butterfly. I will continue to spread my wings and fly.

SOFIA

We all have a journey we travel down to get to where we want to be. Our journeys are told however we want to tell them and this is how I am choosing to tell some of my journey.

Being the youngest of five, I was always told I would take care of my mother. My older brothers and sisters would always say that since I was the one who received the most attention from her, I am the one she didn't abandon, I was the one she took everywhere with, I am the one who got whatever she wanted, then I was responsible for my mother in old age. My mother used to say I would always be with her, that when I was older she would enroll me in a convent so that I would never marry. I considered that a misconception in my immediate family and they knew it. Although I did have my mom around more than they did, my experience with her still left a mark in me that determined the route I took. In middle school, things changed very quickly for me. I was forced to grow up to a maturity level I didn't know I had in me.

A smile can hide so much of what is really going on with a person. In middle school, I discovered the value of a smile and being able to be strong. It is incredible to think that growing up we see the world very one-sided. I thought I was the only one going through life with hardships, until I made friends in AVID. During this time, my brother decided to join the marines. The three older siblings were already married with children, we were the last two single ones, and he decided to serve our nation for four years. In my brother's process to join the marines, our father was deported. Our father has always struggled with drugs and my mother never let us forget that, unless, of course, he was deported. My mother and

I were living alone together. With my father's deportation, my mother would go visit him and I spent many days at my older sister's house. She became like a mother to me. This was the first time I ever got an F in my education. There was so much going on at home, with my mom trying to bring my dad back, and my brother joining the marines, I had a difficult time concentrating on school. My sister motivated me in a positive way to do well in school; it is from her that I learned that if I wanted to be anything in life, my route was going to be getting an education.

    I had to see what my mother went through with my father being deported. He was our main provider; therefore, my mother had to get more hours at work to provide for us. She was so reliant on him that this woman, who would argue with him every day, was dying for him to come back when he was deported. We didn't need him. She knew it. We were doing just fine without him, but she wanted him back. When I saw this, I knew that was not the life I wanted; I will not be dependent on a man to support me.

During high school, I was in AVID all four years. Throughout this time, my brother was deployed to Iraq twice, and our father came back. My brother's deployment to Iraq was a very difficult time for my mother, in turn, it became an even more difficult time for me. She relied on me for emotional support. With my father back, my mother went back to being the home-maker (although she would work weekends). She would make breakfast, lunch and dinner for her husband, not her daughter. I can't deny that money was not something I struggled with. I was not living in luxury, but I was not suffering either. However, I did not like the situation at home, with them arguing and me being placed at the middle of their arguments. When my grandfather (my mom's dad) passed away my sophomore year, I witnessed a whole different person in my mother. He was the first close person to me to pass away, and it was a very difficult time for the family. This event allowed me to see my mother in a new perspective. I saw the child in her and it brought us closer together.

At age seventeen, I graduated from high school and moved out of my mother's home. By age eighteen I was financially self-dependent. I know I am very lucky I did not have to go through being financially self-dependent sooner, but this is my story.

My mother can be a hard person to deal with but she is our mother and has a special place in all of my siblings' hearts. No one can cook like she can; no one can make us laugh at the things she makes us laugh at. My older siblings have forgiven her for leaving them without her asking for forgiveness. That is why my nephews and nieces get to grow up with a grandma. Since I was the youngest and the one to spend the most time with my mother, I became her confidant. I'm the one she calls when she needs to complain about any of my siblings, even about me. When I left her home, the dynamics of our relationship changed.

Never have I heard an I love you, un "te quiero" from her, until I left. My transition into the university was very difficult. I wouldn't be where I am if it wasn't for my experience with my family, AVID, special people in high school including friends and EOP. EOP Summer Bridge, as I always say, allowed me to find my family away from home. I felt a sense of belonging through EOP, and I was motivated to be more involved. Now, as a university graduate, I can't imagine having attended anywhere else for my undergraduate degree except CSU Channel Islands. When I first began in the university I had my mind set on a psychology major and a Spanish minor. However, through my involvement as a University Experience Associate, an EOP Peer Mentor and my volunteering in LEAP I realized what I want to do is promote higher education. I no longer want to be a therapist, and I love Spanish, so I made it my second major instead of a minor. I want to work with the underrepresented communities and I want every child that I cross to know that higher education is an option for them, if that is what they choose to do. My experience in the university has not just been about learning the material I am studying, but growing as a person. I have been challenged academically, emotionally, and all the way around. I have had the opportunity to travel (Cuba, New Jersey, New York) and I learned that I love it.

As for my future, I will continue to further my education. If there is one thing this world cannot take from you, it is your education. I plan to continue on to a master's program, maybe even a PhD. Who knows maybe I will even be the provider for my mother, but I will get to make that decision. My journey is not over; I am still writing this story.

SARINA

The college experience is neither singular nor linear. Through six years of my undergraduate career, I experienced growth, failure, the unknown, achievement, travel, acceptance, and perseverance. The most impactful moments from these years include my first steps on campus as an incoming first year, to my last as a graduate.

I was raised in Claremont, CA, a small college town. Claremont was a community that celebrated education, and I became marinated in such a value. In a single parent household, my two sisters and I grew up side by side, not knowing we fell below the poverty line, because our minds and lives were rich. My childhood reflected a time when my mother worked three jobs, endlessly pursuing a better life for her children. I called a run-down, slumlord apartment "home," and believed that Top-Ramen was the norm. My childhood and environment pushed me to develop a sense of creativity and imagination. My dollhouses were crafted out of books and my playground was an industrial lot. I learned the value of a dollar and the true meaning of less is more. Most importantly, my background instilled tolerance and compassion within me, and taught me to not judge others based on their own backgrounds- for even the most beautiful things can grow between the cracks of a sidewalk.

My father, an addict and thirteen-time felon, has been incarcerated for the majority of my life. Being raised in a community where my school peers had both parents, lived in large houses, and were not on a free lunch program, I had tried so hard to disassociate from what my father's reality meant. I rejected him, my Mexican culture, and in so many ways, my individuality to fit the norm.

My elementary, junior high, and high school years passed. Through those years, my mother emphasized that going to college was a must. As I grew older, my mother explained why we had moved to Claremont- to give me my best chance. She fought every day for me to not become another predetermined statistic from which I stemmed. She was my ignition as I took solace in books, found soccer, aligned myself with unconditional friends, and pursued the opportunities before me.

During my junior year of high school, I learned of the Regional Occupational Program (ROP) and the various vocational training programs they offered free to high school students. By the time I graduated high school, I had completed the ROP *Health Careers I* and *II* course, received my medical assistant certification, and obtained my certified nursing assistant license. The ROP medical field experiences pushed me to desire a Bachelor's of Science in Nursing upon the start of my undergraduate degree come Fall 2011.

As I dived into my college applications with uneasy footing, my high school librarian encouraged me to apply to the Educational Opportunity Program (EOP). We had discussed my family's lack of higher education history and our financial struggles as she explained that I was a first generation college student. I had never heard of EOP, nor understood the importance of such a program. She helped me complete my application, and over the years to come, I would learn that EOP was one of the most critical aspects to my academic and personal success. In the midst of college application acceptances and rejections, I received my letter of acceptance to California State University Channel Islands- It is hard to forget a feeling of validation and possibility. A short time after, I received acceptance from CSU Channel Islands EOP, which finalized my letter of intent to enroll at CSUCI.

As part of CSUCI's incoming first year orientation in June 2011, all accepted EOP students were required to stay extra days for Summer Bridge. Summer Bridge consisted of several workshops, activities, and resources aimed at facilitating the transition from high school to college. We met faculty, learned about student resources, became familiar with different departments, received assistance with scheduling classes, and interacted with the Peer Mentors who guided us. Aside from the academic activities, Summer Bridge encompassed personal and emotional workshops too. For once, I was in a community of students who had similar life experiences to my own. Friendships were made as we shared personal accounts of our challenges, successes, and roots. Connection blossomed through adversity. Summer Bridge was transformative for me as I was faced with myself, and all the years of self-rejection. The powerhouse EOP leaders and students showed me what it was like to embrace our experiences, move on from our pasts, and celebrate education. Because of EOP, I started my first semester in Fall 2011 with academic and personal support, as well as a sense of confidence I had never felt before.

    I was so excited to live and learn in a new location as I began my journey to the nursing program and fulfill my dream of becoming a nurse. The prerequisite courses were difficult, impacted, and time consuming. It was not until I found myself failing my Anatomy and Chemistry courses that I realized nursing might not be right for me. I tried to utilize the tutoring resources on campus, but often felt defeated by the looming thought that I'd never become a nurse. I felt defeated as I noticed my GPA dropping, not reflecting my good grades in high school. After many months of contemplation, retaken courses, and ranging advice, I decided to change my educational trajectory. I dared to declare "undecided" as my major for the time being, and continued to take my general education requirements. From a university critical thinking course to my first American literature course, I finally felt a connection to my curriculum. I found excitement in writing and returned to my early love of books- gaining a new appreciation and understanding of literature. Many visits to faculty office hours encouraged me to pursue an English degree, reigniting my ambition and future goals.

In 2013, I was encouraged to apply to a CSUCI service-learning course, the Juvenile Justice Education Program. I was accepted and through the JJEP, I worked with incarcerated youth, ages

14-21, at the Ventura County Youth Correctional Facility. JJEP provided mentoring and tutoring sessions to the youth, and often engaged in creative work through art. I found myself learning about issues such as the way the United States criminalizes addiction, mass incarceration and the privatization of prisons, poverty and the school-to-prison pipeline, and especially, recidivism, the cycle of an offender's consecutive return to prison. My participation and dedication to JJEP made me curious about my own connection to incarceration, and allowed me to reconsider my father. I continued my involvement with JJEP until 2016.

By being a JJEP participant, I was able to apply for a volunteer position with an affiliated program, the Prison Education Project (PEP), formed at CAL POLY Pomona. As a PEP volunteer, I travelled to the east African country of Uganda in the summers of 2014 and 2015 to teach social business and creative writing workshops. My students were incarcerated men and women of the Luzira Upper Maximum Security Prison and the Luzira Women's Prison. Inside the prisons, the conditions were devastating to witness. Food, medical, hygienic, and educational items suffered. Despite prison politics and lack of resources, education was celebrated and yearned for in those walls. Although I was a teacher in the prisons, my experiences made me a student. I learned about the human spirit in captivity, became connected to my students through writing and discussions, and confronted my misconceptions about incarceration. It was prison education that dismantled my barriers and allowed me to humanize a population that I may not have ever been able to. Education served as a tool to create dialogue with a system I did not want to associate with, and with circumstances I had previously looked down on. I have experienced education as a necessity in forming relationships with those that we are so quick to deem as the other. EOP, JJEP, and PEP empowered me to interact with the prison system in a proactive and positive manner. The societal and correctional issues I became intrigued by, challenged, erased, and eventually reconstructed my diluted understanding of prison and my father.

My college experience was full of struggle: not always having the financial means, working several jobs, being lost in educational pursuit. Despite such, I dedicated the remaining semesters as an undergraduate to academic achievement, civic engagement, and personal growth. My time at CSUCI is highlighted by participating in reading celebrations, various in-state and out-of-state conference presentations, research communities, and being awarded the EOP Service Award ('15),

Student Assistant of the Semester ('16), and a Campus Compact Newman Civic Fellow ('16). The lessons I learned, network of mentors/faculty/friends expanded, and the professional experience I gained through on and off-campus work, is irreplaceable. By time I graduated in May 2017, I had moved back to Claremont and had been working for eight months as a Counselor at a residential treatment facility for teen girls. Currently approaching my one-year anniversary as a Counselor, I continue to see how interwoven poverty, addiction, incarceration, and the foster system are. Many of the youth I work with remind me how similar we all are, just as the Ugandan incarcerated students did.

  In the upcoming months I plan to apply to graduate school in order to begin Fall 2018. As I determine the best course of study for me, I hope to pursue either fields of correctional social work or nonprofit grant writing. My professional passions have proven to include prison work as well as writing. I hope in either role I am able to have a profound impact on incarceration either through case management, or by securing the funds which make prison-minded nonprofits possible.

      My goals significantly transformed over the six-year course of my undergraduate experience. Through every fall, rise, twist, and turn, the Educational Opportunity Program supported and guided me. I never felt alone, even in my times of defeat. I would not be the college graduate I am today without the assistance I received from EOP and CSU Channel Islands. I am eternally grateful. *EOP for life*.

AARON

I graduated May 2017, with a Bachelor's Degree in Communication. I want to take this time to tell you a little about my story and journey to graduation.

I grew up in South Central Los Angeles, and I am a proud son of a single working mother. After my parents got divorced, my childhood took a turn, and I had a lot of growing up to do. Thankfully, my mother was strong and managed to raise three young boys with the help and support of my grandparents. Growing up in South Central isn't the safest place, but I managed. I attended what people call "inner city" schools, and experienced ripped textbooks, students not caring, fights, gangs, drugs, and so much more. However, I didn't let all these exposures influence my future. In middle school, school seemed way too easy. My learning consisted of completing workbooks, handouts, and the majority of the time, we did nothing. This isn't to say that the entire school wasn't learning, there were just those teachers who weren't in it for the students. Every year we had fresh new teachers straight out of their credential or graduate work, and at first they tried their absolute best to teach us, the environment just didn't work with them. It seemed that many of these teachers lost their passion and didn't care and many gave up. Class time went from learning, to fighting each and every day. I didn't feel challenged and I didn't feel like I was learning and I knew I was capable of so much more.

Therefore, I made the decision to ask my mom to let me attend school elsewhere, away from the "ghetto" as we called it. She agreed and I filled out multiple open enrollment forms. When august came, my mom and aunt rode the metro with me to my new high school in North Hollywood and they taught me how to commute to school. In order to get to school every day, I woke up at 4:40 a.m., got ready, and headed out to the metro. I would take the metro blue line and red line commuting all the way to North Hollywood every day. To get back home, I would take the metro red line, blue line, green line, and a bus that dropped me off down the street from my house. The metro became my best friend while in high school and was where I got time to reflect on my life.

    Going to school in a different area was not an easy adjustment. I finally was challenged in school, I was on a quarter system, and found myself second guessing my work. Seeing my middle school friends have it easy made it tough for me at first, especially since I had no friends the first couple of weeks. Although I was challenged, I tried even harder. I spent time on the metro reading for class, doing a lot of homework, and finally felt like I was learning. The teachers cared about my education and pushed us all to do more than what was expected.

While taking the metro was sometimes a drag, I didn't let it stop me from being involved in school. I ended up playing volleyball after school and began getting home around 8 p.m., and still managed to do homework. I joined the Associated Student Body and eventually worked my way up to become senior class president my senior year. The counselors joked about how I hardly ever missed school, was the first to arrive and last to leave, every day. I finally felt like I was worth it and that I was smart.

That feeling was again challenged my entire senior year. I will never forget the day a teacher made me feel less when she told our class that some of us attending college would still never make it in life. That scared me. However, I had more support from my counselors, and other teachers who genuinely believed in me.

It was senior year that I learned about a program called EOP. My counselor made sure I applied and I even helped others apply. I still remember the day I received my acceptance into EOP at CSU Channel Islands. I was riding the metro home, and immediately filled out the form in worry I wouldn't be one of the first to accept the offer. Little did I know that rush to fill out the form would change my entire life.

Stepping foot at CSUCI's Island View Orientation gave me that feeling everyone talks about. I knew it: I was home! EOP Summer Bridge was an experience I will never forget. I met new people from different backgrounds but we all shared something in common. I bonded so much with my peer mentor, Marisol (shout out to Marisol!) that she inspired me to want to become like her and mentor students like me. And I sure did...

Being a peer mentor for three years changed my life completely. Every year the students were so different, yet so alike, and I loved being their support system. The guidance and support I received from EOP reflected through me as a peer mentor every year. EOP allowed me to flourish, believe in myself, and even helped me find and accept things about myself.

I never imagined graduating from a four-year university. I had all odds against me, like the statistics show, I wasn't supposed to make it... but I did. I share my story not as a means to feel sorry, but to show everyone that even those who have everything against them can make it. I owe it all to my family, and my EOP family.

Thank you for sending me that acceptance email years ago. Thank you for giving a kid from south central Los Angeles a chance to prove what he is capable of. Thank you Kari for guiding me every year, and believing in me when I felt like I couldn't keep going. Thank you. Thank you to all the EOP students whether I was your mentor or not, you all taught me the value of having a strong support system and you all made an impact in my life even if you don't know it. To California State University Channel Islands, I thank you for opening your doors and welcoming me home. Finally, to my mom and family, thank you for always pushing me to do better and to go to school. My journey to and through college was rarely easy, but I live by the motto that smooth seas never make a skilled sailor.

Glossary

Defined below: terms and/or acronyms that appear throughout the students' autobiographies.

Advancement Via Individual Determination (AVID): a global nonprofit organization dedicated to closing the achievement gap by preparing all students for college and other postsecondary opportunities. Established more than 35 years ago with one teacher in one classroom, AVID today impacts nearly 1.5 million students in 46 states and 16 other countries/territories.

Educational Opportunity Program (EOP): EOP at California State University Channel Islands provides college access to first-generation students whose educational and economic circumstances have limited their college opportunities. EOP aids in the success of students by providing a comprehensive program of active and targeted support aimed at increasing graduation rates and individual empowerment.

EOP Application Reader: Current CI students that are hired to assist in the process of reviewing EOP applications using a standard rubric to help EOP staff determine the eligibility of incoming student's admission to the program.

EOP Peer Mentor: Continuing CI students that are hired to assist during the EOP Summer Bridge program. Responsibilities include being a mentor for incoming freshman, leading small groups/activities, and serving as representatives of EOP and CSUCI. EOP Peer Mentors provide our incoming EOP class with support and resources to prepare for the rigors of university work.

Leaders in Education Awareness Program (LEAP): LEAP was designed and launched in 2006 to address the interest of CSU Channel Islands students in exposing K-8th grade students in Ventura County to the college exploration process. Each semester, CSUCI student volunteers are selected to participate in this rewarding and prestigious community outreach experience. LEAP student volunteers are known for their commitment to community service, love for children and especially for their dedication to CI. Many LEAP volunteers are the first in their families to attend college and understand the barriers that first-generation, low-income students face.

Prison Education Project (PEP): A project that expands educational opportunities for inmates in 12 California correctional facilities. Volunteers provide academic, life skills, and career development programing. PEP aims to educate, empower, and transform the lives of incarcerated individuals. The goal of PEP is to create a "Prison-to-School Pipeline" and provide in-custody students with the cognitive tools necessary to function as productive citizens.

Summer Bridge (SB): The Summer Bridge Program was established in 2004 to provide an orientation to college life, review basic skills, and provide academic advisement to incoming EOP students. Through a residential program, Summer Bridge assists incoming freshmen with needed support as they prepare for the rigors of university work. Summer Bridge focuses on mathematical skills, creative reading and writing, study sessions and tutorials, and other activities that are part of the full Summer Bridge experience. Participants benefit from personalized attention, individualized instruction and accessibility to campus resources.

University Experience Associates (UEAs): CI students that help facilitate new students' transition to the "University Experience." UEAs provide students with resources, inside and outside of class, that enable them to excel at a four-year institution and beyond.

Made in the USA
San Bernardino, CA
23 April 2019